Caitlen
from
Edna 1984

The Color Nature Library

KITTENS

By
DAVID GIBBON

Produced by
TED SMART

CRESCENT BOOKS

INTRODUCTION

Text books, encyclopaedias and such like have a rather dismissive way of dealing with subjects we have a great interest in which, whilst being entirely factual, leave us with rather a flat feeling. As an example of what I mean, I find in such a book, under the heading 'Cats' the following definition: 'the generic name for all quadrupeds of the Digitigrade section of the carnivorous order, from the lion down to the domestic cat'. There is no doubting the scientific truth of the description but, by its very nature a book such as the one in which I found this description has to generalise, and if there is one thing you cannot generalise about it is cats and their kittens.

I do not propose to go into the question of the evolution of the 'Digitigrade section of the carnivorous order,' or into the relationship between the large cats, lions and tigers, and the domestic cat. The purpose of this book is to deal primarily with the domestic cat and its relationship with us, the people who think we own one of these graceful creatures, and above all with our relationship with their less graceful but very endearing offspring.

It has been argued that man has a subconscious feeling of inferiority, a fear of rejection, in his relationships with his fellow men and that this is one of the prime reasons why he seeks the companionship of animals with which to share his life. Whether this is true or not it is certainly the case that, however rejected he may be, (and sometimes with justification) if he has an animal, a pet dog or cat, waiting for him at home then he knows that here at least he will not find such rejection. Once inside his own home he knows that his companion will accept him for what he is, without question. It is also true to say, surely, that man has a great desire to feel needed and, whilst he looks for fulfilment of this desire in, primarily, his fellows he knows that he is not unique amongst them in this respect and that he is just one of millions all sharing the same need. Such knowledge alone, whether consciously considered or not, is sufficient to promote a feeling, however vague, of insecurity, and to tend to make him look elsewhere for reinforcement of this basic need. In the unquestioning, uncritical companionship of the animals man takes into his home and in the peculiar vulnerability of the young animal in particular, he finds at least in part, the fulfilment he craves.

This kind of reasoning does not however, wholly establish the foundations of the complex relationship between man and his feline companion. In the past cats were kept primarily for their prowess as hunters. At one time there was hardly a home without its 'mouser' but then, there was hardly a home without its mice! In those days cats were almost essential in keeping down the vermin population, and they certainly earned their keep. This natural hunting instinct is something that can distress a number of people. The problem seems to be that, because a person owns a cat it generally follows that they are fond of all animals and the sight of a cat apparently torturing a small animal or bird quite needlessly is something that appears, on the surface, to be an extremely unpleasant and cruel trait. The fact remains, however, that a cat is a hunter, and what is seen as unnecessary cruelty is more likely simply the cat practising its skills in the only way that it can. That cats take a pride in their ability as hunters may be seen in the way they will often 'present' their prey to their masters or mistresses by carefully leaving the corpse outside their door. In this almost ceremonial 'presentation' lies the essence of the cat's attitude to man: having captured his prey in the full spirit of independence and self-sufficiency, he then offers it up as a token of his affection and as a plea for loving approval.

Cat ownership does not require the purchase of a licence. It is not easy, therefore, to arrive at an exact figure for the cat population at any one time. Nevertheless, the best estimates seem to indicate that cat ownership is increasing whilst, at the same time, dog ownership is decreasing slightly. This does not, of course, mean that dogs are no longer popular. What it does highlight is that present social and economic conditions, amongst other factors, are more conducive to the ownership of cats than dogs. So many of the small houses in our cities have now disappeared, to be replaced by high rise blocks of flats, in which the ownership of dogs is almost invariably discouraged if not forbidden and, in any case, is inconvenient for both the dog and the owner. The cost of feeding all but the smallest dogs is considerably higher than the cost of keeping a cat as many owners of large dogs have found, to their surprise. In such situations, those of us for whom the companionship of a pet is something we do not want to forego, find that a cat is the ideal answer. Apart from feeding, and affection a cat can very largely be left to its own devices, something which can be very important if the owner is out at work all day, and in return can, and invariably will, give the greatest amount of pleasure.

Left, Long-haired tabby and white kitten.

The cat has always had something of an air of mystery about it. Even its origins are obscure. It is obviously related to the 'big cats' but the domestic cat was certainly well known to the ancient Egyptians, to whom they rendered great service by helping to control the rats and mice that infested their grain stores. It is also known that the Egyptians worshipped the cat as divine, and were, as far as is known, the only people to do so. It would be a mistake to make too much of this, however, as the Egyptians treated many other animals as divine and most of their Gods had some animal characteristic attributed to them, the jackal and the cobra being but two of the more obvious examples. Many animals were mummified by the Egyptians, including cats and mice; the latter presumably to provide food for the cat on its journey to the other world!

Above, Long-haired black kittens.
Right, Long-haired blue cream kitten.
Left, Long-haired cream and marmalade.

The deification that the Egyptians afforded the cat proved to have disastrous consequences for the animal during the middle ages in Europe. The cat was, by this time, firmly established as a domestic pet but its ancestry of Godliness, and therefore its association with good and evil had by no means been forgotten. These were very superstitious times and anything unusual was very quickly pronounced to be witchcraft or the work of the Devil. There were other factors that also worked to the disadvantage of the cat. Inevitably a large number of the women who were regarded as witches were older women living alone, almost as recluses, and it was extremely likely that they would keep one or more cats as companions. Coupled with this was the cat's natural air of mystery, the eyes, the silent movements and the habit of staring at people as though assessing them. Cats have always produced an allergy in some people. Properly known as aileurophobia, it usually takes the form of causing sneezing, and breathing difficulties, in those afflicted – even when the cat is nowhere in sight. To a superstitious people, beset by fears of witches and demons, all these things must have very quickly convinced them that the cat, far from being an ordinary animal, must be possessed of supernatural powers! The consequence of all this was that the poor cat was hounded and persecuted every bit as much, if not more, than the unfortunate owners. Many cats were put to death along with their mistresses, and many more were chased and killed, or burnt as sacrifices, by mindless mobs.

Even today cats, particularly black cats, figure prominently, at least as cut-outs or drawings, in Hallowe'en celebrations and there is hardly a story published for children in which a witch appears that does not also feature a black cat as her 'familiar'. Given that cats, for entirely the wrong reasons, were, and to some extent still are, associated with witchcraft, it is not difficult to imagine why it is the black cat that figures so strongly in this context. In those 'dark' ages lighting was either non-existent, or of very poor

Left, Bicoloured short-haired kitten.
Right, Long-haired ginger kitten.

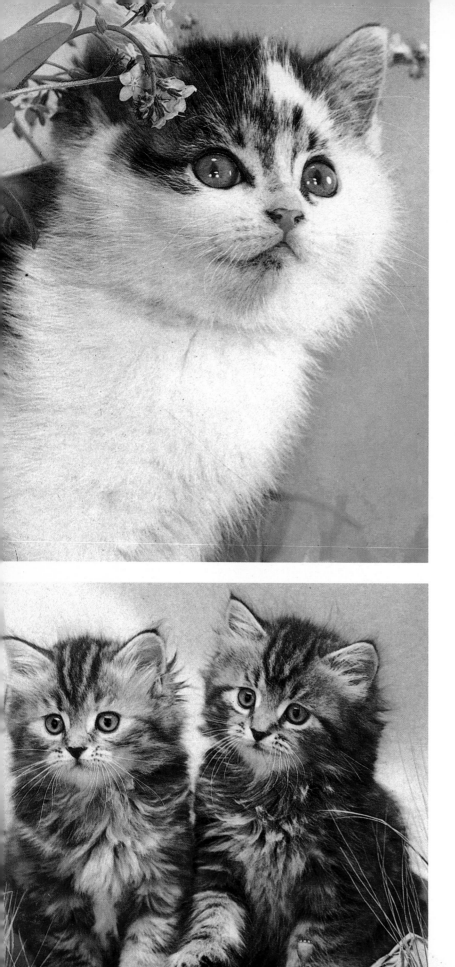

quality, and witchcraft and sorcery were invariably associated with night-time. In such a situation a black cat would hardly be seen at all, except for the eyes which, with their retinas reflecting the light of torches, would appear to shine with what the onlookers could easily convince themselves was an unearthly glow. To be fair, the sight of a black cat with shining eyes and arched back, spitting furiously in the half light, is a rather unnerving sight at the best of times and to those ill-educated people it must have been quite terrifying!

The ability that cats have, in the minds of many people, to evoke a feeling of supernatural forces or even, sometimes, of terror – which may well be a leftover from those dark ages – is something that film producers have put to good use, many times over, in the making of particular films. Whilst this is very understandable from the film maker's point of view, and he is, after all, merely triggering something in the minds of the viewers, it seems rather unfair on the poor cat! A great number of those who declare a disliking for cats in general must have such feelings reinforced, if not occasionally introduced, by the dramatic uses to which cats are put in books, theatres and cinemas. That such feelings are quite irrational is obvious to anyone who owns a cat or knows the animals well. A cat is simply a cat, no more, no less. It does not seek to imitate anything and all its actions are purely catlike.

The popularly held belief that 'a cat has nine lives' means that enormous luck is attributed to the animal at the expense of recognizing the truth of the matter; that the cat is possessed of extraordinary reflexes coupled with superb co-ordination between mind and muscle. It is this that allows them to escape from all sorts of seemingly impossible situations rather than mere luck. The remarkable thing about the cat's physical prowess is just how little real exercise they seem to need in order to stay in such good condition. Even after long periods of inactivity reflexes appear to remain unimpaired and judgement and timing are as good as ever.

Above left, Long-haired tabby and white kitten.
Left, Long-haired tabby kitten.
Right, Long-haired white kitten.

Because of their abilities as hunters and their air of independence, it is sometimes thought that cats can fend entirely for themselves, living on the food that they catch and finding shelter wherever it is available. This, however, is quite incorrect. The domestic cat has been domesticated for far too long for it to be able to look after itself completely. Cats need people and a comfortable home. They need to be fed a proper diet and to have a warm place to sleep, and they need affection. Most people who have travelled to any extent on the continent will have seen examples of the pitifully thin and unkempt homeless cats that try to support themselves, sometimes with equally emaciated kittens, and will know how obviously necessary it is to look after a cat properly.

There are a number of anomalies concerning cats, as indeed there are with so many things in life. They are themselves creatures of great contradictions; at times apparently lazy in the extreme and yet capable of great athleticism; giving every indication of being totally uncaring about the humans with whom they share their lives at one moment, and curling up on someone's lap, purring with contentment, at the next. In many parts of England a black cat is considered to be lucky and appears on postcards and so on, together with a horseshoe, as a symbol of good luck. Only in a few counties are they thought to be unlucky, whereas in the United States the reverse is largely the case.

It might be thought that cats rarely meet each other except to either mate or fight and yet there are well documented instances of them using a common meeting place to do neither of these things but simply spend time in the company of other cats, apparently enjoying some kind of social get-together!

Although cats, as I have mentioned already, are thought of as mysterious and, in some contexts, sinister they are also the most popular cartoon, comic, and pantomime characters. Felix the Cat, Korky, Sylvester, Puss-in-Boots,

Above left, Cream Persian kittens.
Left, Blue-point Persian kittens.

and Dick Whittington's cat seldom fail to find great appreciation and affection from younger readers and audiences. Perhaps the reason is that, as children, we find very few things or creatures mysterious or sinister but simply accept them for what they appear to be, whereas when we grow up we start to read, and to listen to older people, and then realise that we were wrong all the time! We are all obviously creatures of our own civilizations and, as we get older we simply accept its conventions without question. Little girls are not expected to like frogs, toads, mice, or insects and so they almost invariably develop a fear and dislike of them, whilst little boys develop the reverse characteristics, they are expected to like messing about in ponds, hunting for tadpoles, have a matchbox or two in their pockets containing various insects and so, by and large, that is exactly what they do!

People in all walks of life own cats. There is, however, a quite distinct leaning, on the part of writers, poets, actors, and even politicians, towards cat ownership. Apparently Doctor Johnson was very fond of his pet cat, which must have proved rather a trial at times for Boswell who was, it is understood, allergic to them! Possibly one of the major attractions that cats hold for such people is that they are so undemanding; they allow you to get on with what you are doing without interruption and they seem to have an air of contemplation about them which may be well suited to a particular type of person.

Despite its air of the contemplative, the supernatural, even the godlike being, the time inevitably comes when the cat will obey its wholly natural instincts and seek a mate. Domestic cats reach sexual maturity at about ten months and sooner or later the female cat or 'queen', unless she has been 'neutered' will take a romantic moonlit stroll and find herself courted to the accompaniment of that all too familiar 'yowling' and much fighting amongst the toms. Then, if the encounter is successful, begins the quest for a

Right, Short-haired marmalade kitten. *Overleaf*, Long-haired tabby and white kittens.

proper nesting site. The prospective mother searches diligently for a secluded, dry, dark, sheltered spot, preferably with a cover. In the free-living cat this can be a hole in the ground, a hollow tree or a cave as it is in the case of its larger relatives, and she will hunt from such a site within a two mile radius. The domestic cat, in a sense less limited in her choice, frequently seeks out drawers, cupboards, suitcases or…a particular favourite…the spare bed. It may be wise therefore, to make the choice for her and set aside a specific nesting place which is dark, secluded and, above all draught-free. This latter requirement is of the utmost importance for the welfare of the newly born kittens as they are particularly susceptible to draughts. The bed should be provided with some form of disposable material, even paper will do, to cover her blanket so that it can be destroyed once the kittens have been born.

Many misapprehensions are associated with the number of kittens in a litter and it can of course vary from cat to cat. Plutarch maintained that the queen bore one kitten in her first litter, two in her second and so increased the number with each kittening until she bore twenty-eight, significantly the same number as the revolutions made by the moon. This is one of the reasons why cats have also been considered an emblem of the moon. More realistically however, the average litter size over all breeds is four–six kittens, although it is not unknown for the domestic cat to become the proud mother of thirteen in one litter. Should any of the kittens be born dead they must be removed straight away and disposed of. In the event that any of the kittens are not wanted they should on no account be simply taken away and drowned. It used to be quite common for this to happen but drowning causes quite unnecessary suffering, whatever the age of the creature, and it is far preferable to take the kittens to a Veterinarian and have them painlessly put to sleep. If none of the kittens are

Above left, Long-haired tabby and cream kittens.
Left, Long-haired blue and cream kittens.
Above right, Long-haired tabby kitten.
Right, Long-haired cream kittens.

born alive for some reason then, again, it would be wise to take the mother to the Vet as she will be producing milk for her offspring which will not be used, and he will be able to remedy the problem.

Hopefully, of course, the kittens will all be born healthy even though they are initially blind, deaf and very helpless. They will immediately start looking for food from their mother and will be perfectly well looked after by her until they are ready to be removed altogether from her care at the age of two to four months. During the first few days the mother cat stays with her offspring almost constantly and it should be borne in mind that during this time she, herself will need particular attention. While she is feeding her family she will need considerably more nourishment than usual and this should take the form of good, protein-rich food such as white fish, chicken, rabbit, liver etc. and of course milk. It is generally supposed that all cats love milk but surprisingly, many actually prefer water to cow's milk. This may possibly be due to the fact that a very large proportion of cow's milk is, in fact water and it does not have the nutritional value of either goat's milk or tinned milk, particularly for a nursing mother or for a kitten being weaned.

After giving birth to her kittens the queen will require rest and it would be wise not to disturb either her or her kittens, certainly for the first few hours after the birth has taken place. Almost immediately after birth the kittens are given their first thorough wash...a process which not only cleans them but also stimulates the circulation...and so begins a lifetime of scrupulous cleanliness. Cats are naturally clean creatures and the mother cat will instinctively train her offspring to be clean. When the kittens start to wander around therefore, it would be as well to take advantage of this instinct and provide a box filled with sand or earth which can be changed every day until the kittens are ready to venture out of doors.

A kitten's games are an unmistakable preparation for the more serious activities of adult life. In its play are all the movements and stances of stalking and attacking its prey.
On these pages, A short-haired tabby kitten.

Kittens at Play

Somewhere between the tenth and fourteenth day, thanks to the careful attentions of his mother, the infant cat, immaculately clean and in full possession of his senses, is ready to venture away from his birthplace into a new and fascinating world. It is then that this tumbling powder-puff creature first encounters chair-legs, human feet and other strange phenomena and then that his antics with cotton-reels, silver paper and even his mistress'

Above, Short-haired black and white kitten.
Left, Short-haired black kitten.

knitting evoke in us that special delighted indulgence. It is difficult at this stage to identify this tiny fluffy creature with the divine being worshipped by the ancient Egyptians or the sinister witches 'familiar', and yet a careful observation of kittens at play reveals that however much they are enjoying their games, their activities are a preparation for the more serious demands of adult life and bear witness to a heritage shared with larger members of the cat family. The little eyes are bright, the haunches tense and tremble, the tiny bodies shiver in an ague of excitement and the extraordinary stiff-legged rushes and prances form the prelude to a highly effective

Above, Short-haired tabby and white kitten.
Right, Short-haired tortoiseshell kitten.

albeit clumsy pounce. With lashing tail and flattened belly one kitten will stalk his littermates, claw at dangling objects in the air or engage in fearsome combat with a ball. A mother cat will join in her kittens' games, encourage them to stalk and scramble all over her, so that when her offspring encounter a live mouse for the first time, they will instinctively use the time-old feline technique of biting its neck, to kill.

This kind of behaviour, because it so strongly indicates that even in its early infancy the kitten is wholly and un-questionably a cat should, I feel, act as a reminder to prospective kitten owners of the responsibilities involved. As is common with most animals, cats are at their most irresistible when they are very young. It is very hard indeed not to find a kitten appealing and this inevitably, as with puppies, leads to a lot of tragedy. It seems quite astonish-ing to me that so many people will buy a kitten, simply because they find it so appealing and not give any considera-tion to whether they really want a cat or not. They find that the adorable little kitten turns into a grown cat, decide that, after all, they do not really want a grown animal and the responsibilities that ownership implies, and the wretched animal finds itself out on the streets, unwanted and uncared for. Both dogs and cats suffer appallingly in this way, and quite needlessly, if only a little thought was given before the animal was purchased. I do not per-sonally think that the issuing of licenses would do a great deal to alleviate the problem; it certainly has not, so far as can be seen, helped greatly in preventing the same thing happen-ing with dogs. Probably one real answer would be to make the initial acquisition of the kitten that much more difficult by not allowing cats or dogs to be sold except by registered breeders who could, perhaps, operate some kind of follow-up procedure, or at least make sure, before any animal was handed over, that the prospective owners were fully aware of what they

Above left, Burmese kitten.
Left, Bicoloured, short-haired kitten.
Right, Short-haired tabby and white kittens.

were embarking upon in deciding to become animal owners. A long term solution that has often been suggested would be to embark on a programme of neutering a large proportion of the male cat population and thereby decrease, drastically, the numbers of unwanted kittens that are born.

The Kitten's good health!

Not an invitation to raise your glass and toast the well-being of your feline companion! Rather, a few words on the general health and fitness of kittens.

In general, cats are very healthy animals providing they are well cared for with regard to food, grooming and a comfortable home. It is, however, essential that a kitten is vaccinated against feline infectious enteritis, usually at two to three months' old. This particular disease is extremely infectious and, even if symptoms are recognized early and treatment started immediately, it is almost always fatal. Obviously the best person to offer advice, to carry out the vaccination and subsequent 'booster' doses, is the vet. It is therefore important to choose a vet in the area, preferably not too far away, in case of emergencies, and who will, from the outset, have a complete record of all treatment given to the kitten and will be in an ideal position to treat the animal, knowing its full medical history.

Unless it is seriously intended that the kitten, when it matures, will breed and that resulting kittens will be properly catered for, it is wise to have the cat neutered. This should take place before six months but again, the vet will advise on the exact timing. In the case of male kittens the operation is very simple indeed. For female kittens it is a little more complex and takes rather longer but, as with the male, the operation has now become very much routine, is quite safe and the kitten will suffer the very minimum discomfort.

Left, Two long-haired cream kittens.
Above right, Long-haired ginger kitten and long-haired cream kitten.
Below right, Two long-haired ginger kittens.
Overleaf, Two long-haired tabby and white kittens.

In addition to eye infections, the symptoms of which are usually readily apparent; closing of the eye, redness, watering etc., obvious injuries such as cuts, grazes or bites which might lead to more serious problems and may result in an abscess are, again, best dealt with by the vet. It is difficult to bandage a cat's wound successfully for two reasons. In the first place the cat has a very loose skin, something which will be readily apparent to anyone who has tried to hold a cat firmly against its will! Secondly, the cat, like most other animals, does not like bandages or dressings and will frequently try to remove them, sometimes even to the extent of taking out stitches!

Simple ailments, particularly worms – both tape and round – and fleas or lice, are comparatively easy to treat and control. There are many preparations on the market to deal with such problems but it is of the utmost importance that only products of a reputable make, and specifically designed for cats, should be used. It cannot be stressed too strongly that unsuitable medicines of any sort should never be given to cats. This is particularly true of preparations designed for humans. Even a simple aspirin, usually the first thing to be taken by people for a great variety of aches and pains, can prove fatal to a cat.

As far as health is concerned, probably the wisest thing to end by saying is – if in doubt about any aspect of the cat's health, then consult the only person properly trained and equipped to deal with it – the vet.

A Feline Disposition

Another possible source of anxiety to the prospective owner of a kitten is its disposition. In addition to overall good health a good disposition is an important criterion for any pet. In the case of cats, disposition varies only slightly between male and female. There are however, distinct differences in intelligence and disposition between the alley cat (or mixed breed) and the pedigree. The mixed breed kitten is of unknown lineage; therefore, its

Above, White Persian kitten and blue Persian cat.
Left, Orange-eyed white Persian cats.
Right, Short-haired cream and short-haired blue cream kittens.
Overleaf, Long-haired tabby kittens.

temperament and disposition are difficult to assess. By chance the mixed breed may prove a happier, healthier and more robust pet than a pedigree. On the other hand, the behaviour and vigour of the direct ancestors of pedigreed cats are indicative of the characteristics the offspring will possess as adults.

The Siamese *on these pages* is one of the most popular breeds. There are a number of varieties, identifiable by the colour of their 'points', (face mask, ears, feet and tail), the four recognised variations being the Seal point, Blue pointed, Chocolate pointed and Lilac pointed Siamese.
Overleaf, White Persian kittens.

Whatever the parentage of the new kittens: whether or not they are pure bred, the kittens themselves will almost certainly be quite adorable. A word of advice however, to the owners of pedigree kittens: Their markings are highly deceptive and many do not acquire their characteristic markings and colours for weeks. For example Siamese kittens are white at birth, while Blue Persians have tabby markings and Black Persians are brown. It is some time before the true physical features of the adult cat really establish themselves and this is possibly why in general an adult, pedigreed show cat begins its career in the 'novice' class, at the age of eight months or older.

Cats on show

The first cat show was held at the Crystal Palace, near London in 1871. Since that time both cat shows and cat societies, often devoted to one particular breed, have flourished. Nevertheless it is true to say that, compared with the vast population of cats throughout the world, the number that are actually shown is relatively small. Apart from cat breeders, to whom the winning of prizes is of obvious importance, most of the people who enter their cats for shows do so very much for the fun and pleasure they get out of the experience. The fact that a cat can be entered for every show for which it is eligible, without ever coming near to winning a prize of any sort, should, of course, in no way diminish it in the eyes of its owner, to whom it will remain the most beautiful cat in the world, and this is as it should be.

The cat makes an excellent mother. If worried by noise or too much activity in the vicinity of her young she will pick them up and carry them one by one to a safer spot. Experiment teaches her as it teaches her counterparts in the wild, to grip her kittens by the scruff of the neck.

Every cat show, except those restricted to only one breed, have different sections for various breeds of cat and range in size, scope and importance from small local events to great shows such as the Olympia National Cat Show. Before entering any cat for a show, whether local or national, it is wise to read carefully all the conditions of entry. With 'serious' shows it is usual for there to be insistence that the cat is registered with the appropriate body and, in all cases, proof is required that the cat has been vaccinated and is healthy. Obviously it would be disastrous if a cat suffering from some infectious disease were to come into contact with a large number of healthy animals and infect them. This was by no means unknown in the early days of cat shows, but is, happily, no longer a problem.

There are very many, and distinct, different breeds of cat but they are normally classified under four main headings; Long-haired or Persian,

Above left and above, Tabby and white cat and litter of kittens.
Left, Black and white cat and litter of kittens.
Right, Tabby and white cat and black and white cat and kitten.

Short-haired (excluding Foreign), Foreign Short-haired (excluding Siamese), and Siamese. Within the first two groups particularly, there are a number of breeds that appear in both, the only real difference being that they have either long or short hair. Under Foreign Short-haired may be found some of the more exotic breeds, such as the Abyssinian, Russian, Burmese, Tonkanese, Havana etc., whilst under Siamese, which might be thought a fairly straightforward classification, there are now such varieties as Tabby-point, Tortoiseshell-point, Red-point as well as the, perhaps, more familiar Seal, Chocolate, Lilac and Blue-points.

In addition to all the recognized breeds of cat there are always sections covering 'any other colour', or 'any other variety'. If it is felt, therefore, that a cat does not fit into any of the distinct breeds there is no need to worry; who knows perhaps a new trend will be set and a new classification introduced, in time, of which your cat could be the first champion!

Left, Long-haired cream and long-haired marmalade kittens.
Right, Long-haired blue cream kittens.
Below, Tortoiseshell and white kitten.

Kittens in Photography

As has already been mentioned, cats, and particularly kittens, are tremendously appealing to look at. The fluffiness of the little animal, its big eyes and general air of inquisitiveness, coupled with the great vulnerability that is so apparent in any young creature, are all ingredients that have been put to exceedingly good purpose by publishers of postcards, greetings cards, calendars, chocolate boxes, and a great number of other commodities that rely on the eye of the prospective purchaser being attracted to the product. This, in turn, has obviously led to a considerable demand for really outstanding photographs, such as many that appear in this book. Whilst it is not too difficult to obtain a fairly passable snapshot of the family pet, good enough to be put in the album and shown to friends, when it comes to providing high quality colour photographs, with the cats or kittens carefully arranged into a pleasing composition that will be suitable for commercial purposes, then it is a very different story. A bowl of flowers, or some other still life arrangement may well be no easy task to set up but, once the elements of the picture are arranged to the photographer's satisfaction, they will at least stay put and give ample time for the photograph to be taken. Not so with kittens, or most other animals for that matter. A kitten, in particular, is very active, inquisitive, mischievous and, perhaps above all, self-willed. Contrary to what anyone may think, it is not really possible to scold a kitten, or punish it in any way, to make it co-operate with a photographer. It has to be a case of patience and then more patience, if necessary adapting the requirements of the

Above left, Long-haired cream and two long-haired ginger kittens.
Left, Long-haired blue cream and long-haired cream kittens.
Right, Cream Persian kitten.

photograph to the wishes of the kitten, rather than the other way around. A frightened kitten or cat will look unmistakably either frightened or hostile in the finished work and no-one will want to use photographs that show this, so any attempt on the part of the photographer to try to impose his will too strongly will prove to be a complete waste of time.

Most, if not all, successful animal photographers have a real understanding of, and with, the animals they use. It would be out of the question to simply take a kitten and place it in a pre-arranged setting and simply take the photograph. That is, unless that was precisely what the kitten wished to do at that particular time – not a very likely or frequent occurrence! It is far

Left, White Persian kitten.
Above, Short-haired cream kittens.
Right, Long-haired blue cream kittens.
Overleaf, Long-haired tabby cat and kitten.

more likely that the photographer will spend some considerable time playing with the kittens, getting to know it and gaining the animal's trust and confidence. Only after this point has been reached will he attempt to place the kitten in the setting he has arranged and watch the kitten's reactions. Often things do not quite work out in the way they have been planned. I have known occasions where the kitten has played for too long and, instead of a lively picture of an alert little animal, the result has been a photograph of a kitten fast asleep! Very appealing, but not what the photographer had in mind and it only remains for the original idea to be tried again when the kitten wakes up. Sometimes, of course, the kitten decides that it simply will not co-operate in any way and the whole idea has to be scrapped and replaced by something else.

It should be remembered that all the foregoing applies primarily to studio photography and that, in such work, large format cameras, of the type that require a dark cloth to be draped over the photographers' head in order that he may see the inverted image of the subject on a ground glass screen, are used. Whilst such cameras are capable of producing quite superb results and are essential in obtaining large transparencies or negatives they do, nevertheless, impose quite severe technical limitations on the photographer. Working at the very close distances necessary with a relatively small animal only a limited amount of the subject can be sharply focused and, in the case of an animal which moves very quickly, this can prove to be an extremely difficult problem to overcome and usually neccessitates the use of high powered flash equipment. In fact the kitten itself is rarely used for the preliminary focusing, this being done quite often by substituting a toy animal of the appropriate size which is removed when all has been made ready, the lighting and so on has been arranged, and is replaced hopefully, by the kitten!

If I have succeeded in highlighting some of the difficulties that can be experienced in photographing a cat or kitten, in the studio, then the added complications of attempting to do the same but with two, three, four or more kittens in the one picture may be

Left, Long-haired cream kitten.

imagined! All the problems are multi-plied by the number of animals, with the addition of trying to get them all to do what is wanted at the same time. Being present at such a time in an animal photographer's studio can be a quite hilarious experience for every-one – except, of course, for the photo-grapher, who is probably wondering what perverse streak in his nature made him take up animal photography at all! With much perseverance, how-ever, things do work out in the end and the feeling of achievement is quite con-siderable. Just how well they work out may be judged from the many photo-graphs of two or more cats and kittens in this book, and such pictures are in themselves a great tribute to the skill and patience of the photographer concerned.

Above, Long-haired marmalade and cream kittens.
Right, Black Persian.

All Friends Together

In their wild state cats are natural hunters and do not make friends easily with other animals. This is perfectly understandable; another animal is either potential food to be hunted, and subsequently eaten, or is a threat to the cat's life and territory and is treated as such. If an animal falls into neither one

Left, White Persian kittens.
Right, Short-haired ginger kitten.
Below, Long-haired cream and long-haired marmalade kittens.
Overleaf, Seal point Siamese kittens.

nor the other of these categories then it is of no interest and is simply ignored. Territory is extremely important to most wild animals. This is not simply because the animal wants to have privacy, but for the very good reason that it is ensuring that an area is available when a family is born in which the offspring will be able to grow, and feed, in comparative security.

When an animal is domesticated and becomes the companion of human beings, to the extent of sharing a place in the family home, it still brings with it

Left, White Persian kittens.
Below and right, Long-haired blue cream kittens.

the instincts of the wild, to a greater or lesser degree. With cats, particularly, it is generally supposed that they do not take kindly to other animals, except other cats, living in the same house. Whilst this is quite true in so far as a fully grown cat suddenly presented with, say, a dog as an additional household pet, would resent the intrusion strongly, it does not mean cats will never live peacefully with dogs, rabbits or other animals. I'm quite sure that there are many recorded instances of cats even sharing their homes with birds, but I do feel that this

Left, Long-haired white kittens.
Above and right, Short-haired marmalade and white kittens.
Overleaf, Long-haired cream kitten and cat.

might be stretching relationships a litttle too far as a normal course!

Should it be decided that, say, a cat and dog are wanted in a home, then it would obviously be the wisest course to get them as puppy and kitten respectively, so that they may grow up in one another's company from the outset. Failing such a possibility, it must be remembered that, in the same way as a child may feel resentment at a new brother or sister if it feels that enough attention is not being paid to it, or it feels, quite erroneously that it is not wanted as much as before the new

Left, Long-haired white and two Seal point Siamese kittens.
Right, Short-haired tabby kittens.
Below, A selection of Siamese kittens with their varying 'points'.

arrival, this is very much the way an established pet will feel about a strange new companion. It is extremely important that the original pet, be it cat or dog, is made to feel wanted and loved as much as it ever was. In fact it would probably be wise to make even more of a fuss of it until it gets quite used to the new pet. Patience is the obvious ingredient in making sure that the new relationship achieves harmony. It must also be made quite clear, from the outset, that both pets have their own beds and food and drink bowls. Under no circumstances is it wise to allow certain behaviour from one animal, and to forbid it to the other. If the cat is allowed to lie on the settee, then it would be quite wrong to stop the dog from enjoying the same privilege, otherwise resentment is sure to build up.

Given the right amount of patience, understanding, firmness and tact, there is no reason at all why different animals, supposedly implacable enemies, should not be the best of friends. There is something particularly charming about such friendships and the owner, of course, gets the best of both worlds in having two different pets to make a fuss of and, in turn, to make a fuss of him or her.

Whenever the idea of a faithful companion, waiting for its master or mistress, is considered, it usually conjures up a picture of a dog, patiently anticipating the sound of the familiar voice or footstep. This is perfectly true, of course. Dogs are much more demonstrative in their greetings than are cats.

Above left, Long-haired white kitten.
Left, Long-haired cream kitten.
Right, Short-haired tabby kittens.

Nevertheless, it would be wrong to think that cats are not interested in the absence, or impending return, of their human companion. I'm sure that most of us have heard of cats waiting, sometimes at the door, or even at the garden gate, ready to offer a 'welcome home' greeting. I recently heard of a cat that goes much further than this and, in fact, behaves very much more like a dog in this respect. The cat lives in a small village and the master travels by train from the local station each day. The cat appears to know, each day, the time that its master will be returning and, at the appointed time, sets out for the station, some two miles distant, and waits for

Left, White Persian kittens.
Above, Long-haired ginger kittens.
Right, Two long-haired ginger kittens and a long-haired cream.

him. This particular car can quite easily pick him out from all the other returning passengers, and does so regularly! Most of the local people know the cat, a Siamese, and it is something of a local celebrity.

Such behaviour is, of course, rather out of the ordinary but, there is no question that, in a happy home, a cat will always be pleased to see its owner, whether it acts in an outwardly demonstrative manner or not.

Part of the secret of establishing a relationship of this kind lies in laying the foundations for it while the cat is still very young. To take a kitten away from its mother and the remainder of the litter too soon may, as some have suggested, eventually result in a neurotic cat and neurosis in cats manifests itself in unpleasant and unpredictable displays of temper, which can only be undesirable. At the same time, if a kitten is left too long with its mother, it may become so strongly orientated towards the animal world that a close relationship with a human master or mistress is unlikely to develop. There can be no hard and fast rule for the timing of removal from the litter...generally it should occur somewhere between the kitten's second and fourth month but the right moment must depend on the development of each individual kitten and on the ability of the prospective owner to understand and recognise it. From that moment onwards, shared experiences, whether they be confrontations over balls of knitting wool or tranquil moments spent together in the light of a flickering fire will create an unbreakable bond. Given a sensitive, mutual understanding, to tumble with your pet on the hearthrug is not to detract from the dignity of the animal but to ensure that the mature cat will become a faithful, if somewhat independent friend.

Left, Long-haired tabby and white kittens.
Above left, Long-haired ginger and white kitten.
Right, Blue-eyed long-haired white kitten.
Overleaf, Long-haired cream kitten.

First published in Great Britain 1979 by Colour Library International Ltd.
© Illustrations: Colour Library International Ltd, 163 East 64th Street, New York 10021.
Colour separations by La Cromolito, Milan, Italy.
Display and text filmsetting by Focus Photoset, London, England.
Printed by Cayfosa and bound by Eurobinder - Barcelona (Spain)
Published by Crescent Books, a division of Crown Publishers Inc.
All rights reserved.
Library of Congress Catalogue Card No. 79-50709
CRESCENT 1979